1

HOW TO GET

RICH QUICK

CONVERT

10K to 100M

Moria MacMegan

First Edition March 2014

ISBN - 13: 978-0615959306
ISBN - 10: 061595930X

Published by: MORIA CORPORATIION
               UNITED STATES OF AMERICA

Artwork by Mark Lawler

BISAC Category: Business & Economics/ Investments & Securities/ Futures

Search keywords: Get Rich, Futures, Make money, Commodity, Pyramid

DEDICATION

This book is dedicated to all those of humankind who would pursue the affluent life on the magnificent God created Earth with free trading markets and personal freedom. May they pursue it with honesty, integrity, and righteousness. May they be generous and kind to their fellow humans. May they help those humans who have needs with wise council, patience, and love; all of this with deep understanding wisdom.

Moria MacMegan
In year of our Lord Jesus Christ 2014
May He come again soon.

Table of Contents

YOUR   PILE?

ONE

INTRODUCTION

This is a book on how to turn $10,000.00 into $100,000,000.00. Inflation has robbed the dollar of its value so in modern 2014 terms more like $30,000 into $300,000,000 --- what we really are talking about is increasing your capital by a factor of 10,000 or 10 to the fourth power.

You will do this by buying and selling futures contracts. They used to be called commodity contracts.

You say it is impossible? I know from experience it can be done. Hillary, You-Know-Who, with some help turned $1000 into $100,000 using cattle futures contracts. Now, of course, there may have been some shenanigans in that operation, but again, I know from experience it can be done. I spent 16 years as a professional registered Commodity Trading Advisor. I made a lot of money for my clients; I lost a lot of money for my clients. I also lost all my money. Needless to say, if I had kept a little of my money I would not be writing this book and offering its wisdom and science and experience to you for very little ready cash. So it will be a great benefit to you that I have lost my money. Now I did not quite lose it all trading futures. I was legally robbed by a huge criminally run saving bank, regulated by the government of the United States of America, but that is another story.

It has been said by some sage,

"If a commodity trader dies rich, he dies before his time."

In my case that is quite true. I am not dead yet and am not rich.

One day as I was reflecting on my life, since I am getting to be an old man, the thought hit me that I very well might leave life on this beautiful Earth without passing on to my grandchildren and other fellow humans the lessons and techniques, which I have kept very secret until now, that which I learned in trading commodity futures contracts during the course of my lifetime. Therefore, you dear reader, and I hope for my sake you at least paid good money for this book, will be the beneficiary of this experience.

If you chose to implement what you will learn in this book and to embark on a futures contract (or now days sometimes called derivatives) trading quest to generate for yourself 100 million dollars or even a billion dollars, it will change your life. And, by that I mean the essence of life itself. You should consider that possibility very carefully. You may be living what to you is a good satisfying life and you may not want to see yourself changed. Your friends may not like you anymore. Your wife or significant other may not think you are the same person any more. Consider these things very carefully.

To successfully trade futures contracts in the manner presented in this book, you will need to be a highly disciplined, focused individual. If you are a liberal or otherwise muddled, deranged thinker or plagued by such insanities, it will change you into a conservative. You may not

INTRODUCTION

like that prospect. Of course, if you succeed in the quest defined in this book, 100 million dollars will, no matter what, change your life, unless, of course, you in fact already have a ready 100 million dollars.

If in journeying on with this quest, you do not succeed in generating the 100M, you still will, in the process of attempting to make the quest, become a changed person. Truth and reality are essential for success in this quest. Undertaking this quest will result in you seeing and understand things as they really are and not what you would have liked them to be. This results in a changed person so that your insanities and deranged thinking must disappear. You will be forced to buy truth and sell error.

This book includes statistics. I have studied the standard college statistic textbooks and taken college courses in such but you should understand a lot of statistics principles presented in this book are not very rigorous, there being no reason to really be so, since we are concerned about what works and makes money and not necessarily in mathematical formality. I have tried to not laboriously use mathematics, but what I do present is necessary for understanding what you are doing. If you do not have theoretical understanding of what you are doing you will have little confidence in what you are doing. Yet confidence is essential in order to succeed. This is not a black box process; however, some things work because they work and not because they are mathematically rigorous.

The goal of this book is to teach you the methods whereby you can conduct a Grand Canonical Pyramid! Hereinafter, let's call it GCP. The GCP in futures contracts can take $10,000 of your money and turn it into $100,000,000. This will not be easy.

The psychological stress of pyramided futures positions can be overwhelming. You are not going to be able to do this overnight. You will be like a long distance runner. You must run a six-minute mile before you run a five-minute mile, and you must run a five-minute mile before you run a four-minute mile.

The first few times you expose your ten grand to this quest you will likely lose it. If you intend to persist, you must learn from the experience. In the end success in all of this is all psychological. These rules work and you will succeed if you discipline yourself, believe in yourself, and don't crack from the stress. To be absolutely sure of success, first practice these rules to build your confidence that they work with very small sums of money. Then have 70 grand available. Try it seven times. There is an almost 100% certainty you will succeed in seven trials given that you execute with diligence and train yourself with great dedication. You are like the athlete heading for the perfect 10. It takes lots of work.

In this book there will be discussion about computers and programs to compute the variables that are herein described. Having someone build these programs could cost you a lot of money. Having the programs would certainly make it very convenient. If you are your own programmer the cost could be minimal. I would recommend that you do all the calculations by hand. That way you get good at it and understand what you are doing. You will learn to make shortcuts and get approximate answers that are almost as good as accurate answers which a computer would generate.

I was raised in a rather poor family so when I became a bright young slightly undereducated theoretical physicist, and an overeducated electronic device development engineer, the first time that I lost 100 grand of my hard earned money, I was sick about it for six months. (This also was when 100 grand was worth much more than it is now.) The next time I lost 100 grand I cried for a week. The third time I lost

INTRODUCTION

100 grand I thought to myself for a day or so, "this hurts." Then when I got into the advisor business and made millions for my clients, and my clients thought me some kind of guru, it was lots of fun. But I did not think about being a guru or enjoy a good thought about it.

There is an old poem that my 7th grade grammar school teacher forced me to memorize. I hated poetry then, especially if I had to memorize it. Its punch line went,

> "Success is failure turned inside out, the silver lining of the cloud of doubt."

That poem created in me a character flaw. That flaw is to never give up. Consequently, I persisted too long in quests that were by all logic going to be failures, while I held irrational hopes for success. That borders on insanity. The really great skill of this whole process is to know when to quit. You do not want to follow your quest until you have destroyed yourself. In pursuit of the Great White Whale, you too, like Ahab, in the tale of Moby Dick, can destroy yourself.

You must keep your wits about you at all times. Logic, mathematics, statistics, health, courage, discipline, a little money, and a tested plan, will not only capture the Great White Whale, but also make you very rich.

You might want to think about whether you really want to become rich. Being rich has its own set of problems. First a cloud of blood sucking attorneys will follow you around seeking to suck as much as they can out of you. And once they suck you dry, even your own lackeys will throw you overboard like an emaciated corpse from a slave ship. Your wife, relatives, friends, and the tax collector will make lots of demands to share your good fortune. Your sons will become playboys and your daughters will become playthings of the rich and famous.

You might think about these things before you begin your quest. If you understood all the ramifications you might decide you do not want to become rich. Jesus taught his disciples to pray,

"Give us this day our daily bread."

Yes, the truth is, daily bread is sufficient for those destined to have ultimate riches; that is, to be with The Lord Jesus throughout eternity.

Wealth piled up slowly day-by-day, and that which has been thoroughly taxed, becomes old money, tucked away in safe things, and it lasts. Wealth accumulated very rapidly, as in a GCP, has a very high probability of disappearing into a wisp of thin air.

But then it has been said by another sage,

"It was better to have loved and lost than never to have loved at all".

If you are going to continue to read this book and implement its directives as a quest for riches,

INTRODUCTION

WELL, GOOD LUCK!

WATCH OUT FOR THE DRAGONS!

VAYA CON DIOS!

TWO

A LITTLE HISTORY

Great ideas and inspirations come; it seems, out of the blue. Perhaps one has been thinking about the general subject for some time, and in a moment of vision, a grand idea is conceived. Then perhaps the vision is lost because of distractions or the press of duty or job or family or friends, and the vision is aborted. My consulting computer programming business usually became very dead during the Christmas/New Year holiday season. The phone just did not ring and most people went out partying. It happened the holiday season of 1970-1971. All the conception of my own commodity trading system started as a vision, became conceived, and was reduced to a procedure during the week between Christmas and New Years.

The System, as I will call it, is a collection of procedures and mathematics. Years later in promotional literature we called it the

"Statistical Qualifier System".

The system has four facets to it. The first is a statistical calculation which produces a "signal"; the second is called, "structure", and is essentially a pattern recognition template; the third a set of trading rules, and the fourth a money management method. There should have been a fifth, which I never conceived, which should have been how the system interacts with the world, and what to do if the world is watching me or now, you.

I have never written this whole thing down before, so as to never have it be lost to posterity, I write it down here. My hope is that I can remember it all. It made me, my family, and my clients a lot of money, and became the defining financial movement of my whole life.

I had been learning a lot about commodities and commodity trading from my dear very close friend and mentor, an extremely fine exquisite quiet gentleman with superb manners, of Jewish ancestry with the name of Paul. Paul was a Military Systems Analyst specializing in the discipline of Operations Research, a discipline conceived to win World War II. At that time he worked for Stanford Research Institute in Menlo Park, California, a contract research facility very loosely associated with Stanford University.

SIGNAL

Paul used a nine day convolution to generate signals. Every day he would calculate a change in a geometric product index of all the futures markets. He never gave me the basic theory of what he was doing. I will give mine later. He would algebraically add up all the open to close differences in the commodities prices and all the close to close daily differences. Paul used one trading tick in wheat as his unit of measure. All the price changes of all the commodity contracts relative to wheat ticks were added up. He then summed up all the price changes as in the number of "ticks". A sum total each day of say, +59, or −179 ticks, as the change from open to close, and then also the change for close to close. Paul's method worked very well as it was a very simple short hand way to compute by hand what he wanted to know, which was --- how did the market as a whole change today? He never told me where he got this system or how he thought it up.

Paul would compare the last nine days of open to close difference as a statistical set. This is a very small sample from which to make any statistical judgment, but one has no choice, as this is all you have. Nine days to Paul was very significant. Why I am not sure. Perhaps it is an approximate two week interval. If the open to close algebraic sum of all the ticks for today compared to those of the last nine days was greater than 1½ sigma then today was called a signal. A buy signal if the change was negative and a sell signal is the change was positive. Therefore, tomorrow would be a day to buy commodity futures contracts or a day to sell commodity futures contracts. Sigma stands for the standard deviation of the nine day set of numbers.

Why open to close rather than close to close? I never figured that out. It just worked.

Paul thought he was measuring the buying pressure going on for the day. The assumption perhaps was that the buying pressure would dissipate the next day and selling pressure would take over.

I was much more mathematical than Paul. What Paul was doing was a differential convolution filter being passed over the day to day data. I was operating on and had access to the cutting edge of computer technology in those days with several user accounts at the Stanford University computer center in Palo Alto, California. I created a geometric index of all commodity contracts. This is a product of all; let's say N, commodity futures contract prices multiplied together. The index then is the n th root of the product of all the prices. The change in the index is the sum of all the partial derivatives of each commodity with respect to the time interval. Or in delta type mathematics the delta I (I being the index) is the sum of the all the changes in the commodity prices. I would use the weighted sum of the last four futures contracts of each commodity. I eventually had the whole thing programmed in Basic (A primitive computer language) on a computer where I could call up and get the information of all the commodity futures prices from a data service provider.

The index changes were input to the Stanford University Computer. I did not think nine days had any special significance so I had the computer calculate 6 day, 7 day, 8 day, etc., etc., up to 12 day intervals. I found that greater than twelve did not seem to have much meaning and that six was problematic because of such a small sample, but I used it anyway. I used the rule that I had to have at least two of this set to be greater than 1.37 sigma to generate a signal. This came about after I did large number of samples and came to the conclusion that I needed a signal on the average every 5 days in order to have meaningful trading with a high expectation of generating money. When I used the rule that any two of the set of six to twelve being over 1.37 sigma created a signal, I got a signal every five days like I wanted on the average. This was done over many years of data. This constitutes the first facet of the trading system, computing a "signal".

What is the meaning of a signal? I have concluded that being forced to act at some point in time greatly assists the decision making process. It forces one to act. The oversold and overbought condition of the market has some significance, but it is very hard to generate some consistent theory as to why what one is doing is meaningful. In the early days I had great confidence in it; I know Paul did. Today I am not so sure. Forcing me to act was probably more or just as important. Also, obviously, in the total randomness of the markets, if the market sold down all day in a very significant way, is not tomorrow a good day to buy? Prices are certainly cheaper in that case than yesterday.

STRUCTURE AND TRADING RULES

The second facet to the System was structure. Little arrows would be placed on a day-by-day bar chart of a commodity futures contract under the day following a buy signal and over the day following a sell signal. I would look at these charts and interpret them according to the set of rules. I will list the set of rules in a subsequent chapter. The rules were such as buy on the third buy signal that is at a higher price level than the last two signals. To buy futures of a commodity the buy signals must hold and not be violated and the sell signals must not hold and be violated for at least three weeks. I could look at a chart and make this judgment. I always wanted to get the computer to make this decision but I never got around to writing the program to do it. It would have been a tedious program to write, as humans in those days were better at pattern recognition than computers. Structure was very important. Structural analysis was done whenever a signal was generated, to decide what to buy or sell, if anything, the next day.

For the third facet a running day after day calculation of the set of open to close prices for each commodity future to be considered for trading was done. From this the standard deviation of the set (hereinafter called sigma) for each futures contract open to close difference in price is calculated by a convolution over the given number set of days. This sigma was used for the get out rules that are based on structure violations. Any futures position price that violated the buy signal on which it was established by ½ sigma was to be liquidated intraday. Once a position was established, any subsequent signal must be violated two days on the close to liquidate the position. A fail safe out, which should be the worst case, is a three sigma violation of any signal. Sigma is again the standard deviation of the price volatility of the individual future, based on the open to close price change. This is computed by a convolution set over any time period. Generally, I used somewhere between nine and 27 days, whatever seemed appropriate. Eventually, after following a futures contract for a while, a nominal value of the sigma can be assumed, and it is used to determine get out points.

MONEY MANAGEMENT

The fourth facet was money management. Paul believed that pyramiding was the only way to make any real significant money. My thinking on the matter is that in any linear system, the buys and sells will generate a statistical normal distribution of results. Since we are dealing with random "white" noise, (the markets themselves in their price changes from moment to moment are random or white noise) any linear system dealing with the white noise will also be white noise. Thus when one employs any linear system, to consistently make net profits one would have to be very good at picking winning candidates for a trade before the trade is to be made.

In the 1970's and 80's and 90's most commodity trading advisors used a moving average system. A moving average is also a convolution of the day to day price movement; in this case, the convoluting function is a rectangular pulse, also called a square function. For example a six day moving average convoluting function would have a value of one the last six days and a value of zero elsewhere.

I came to the conclusion that to consistently perform one must make profits exponentially and not linearly. In my system I decided to made money exponentially and lose money linearly. To do this one must add to positions based on profits. This is called a pyramid.

Pyramiding has the reputation of being very dangerous and has an associated high risk. That is essentially true. The problem then is to control the risk. I eventually settled on a formula where if a position generated seven sigma of profits, I would add to the position. Markets usually do not react more than three sigma in any normal sell off. In fact one of the liquidation rules was that if a market sold off more than three sigma from a new high close, the position was to be liquidated. Also the exchange minimum money margins required by brokerage firms to back the futures positions are generally about three sigma.

A severe problem occurs when the volatility in the market changes. Sometimes a news event or anticipated news event for a price action will cause an increase in volatility. Sigma is a measure of the price volatility and in this writing I use the terms interchangeably. For example, let's say wheat has been trading with a sigma of about three cents for months. News comes out that the Soviets are starving and they start buying wheat in huge quantities and selling their gold. The price of wheat starts to rise rapidly only now the sigma is increasing to five cents. If you were pyramiding with a three cent sigma, and the market now reacts with a normal 15 cent three sigma sell off, the new three sigma, you are going to be wiped out. Thus successful pyramiding must be very sensitive to changes is volatility.

My pyramiding rules required a futures price to be "in the clear", that is no sell signals holding, and required seven sigma in profits to add each new contract. I originally calculated that six sigma would be adequate, but I arbitrarily picked seven to have a little margin of safety. Even then lots of "campaigns", that is serious pyramiding efforts, would end in loses.

The key to successful long term profitability was to treat every new position as a pyramid campaign until the position proved itself a loser. Many, many times, I would add one contract or so and then the position would prove to be a loser and, of course, I would lose more from having tried to pyramid then if I had not tried to pyramid at all.

In order to have pyramid action close to a mathematical continuum one needs to start with five contracts. That is a rather large position for most normal managed accounts, so small managed accounts started with three. With five contracts a price move of three sigma would generate 15 sigma of profits. This, for example, would be enough to add two new contracts if one is adding contracts based on seven sigma of profits. The ideal pyramid campaign would start with a position of five on a buy signal. Usually the price then moves up and down for a while. Sell signals develop above the market and buy signals below the market. Once the price is through the sell signals and is moving up, that is, "in the clear" contracts are added on the trading day close every day seven sigma in profits is generated. If a sell signal occurs, buying is stopped until again the price moves above the new sell signal for two days on the close. On buy signals, contracts can be added with the rule that there must be seven sigma in profits behind every added contract. The assumption has been made that initially seven sigma was behind each contract in the initial trade. In practice, three sigma behind the initial positions was acceptable as managed accounts usually have large amounts of unused funds available.

This is a very dynamic entertaining trading system. My clients used to get very excited when a campaign got serious. Good campaigns have a life from three to six weeks. Sometimes I would have positions go from five to 35 contracts, (35 was the arbitrary maximum I invoked to control very severe risk, being seven times the initial position) and produce huge profits. All one needed was one big campaign a year to generate 50% to 100% gains on the nominal account size for the clients for the year. All the small losses were more than made up by one good pyramid campaign.

It turned out that 63% of my trades were small losers, about 32% were small winners, and 5% significant winners. If I could do that we made 50% to 100% per year on account size.

THREE

SYSTEM DEVELOPMENT

Here is a little history of the system development. I traded my own accounts from the conception of the system in January of 1971 to the fall of 1976. I made a little money and lost a little money, probably a net loser, I do not remember. Nothing serious happened, however, as I was changing things and learning. 1976 was a very tough year for me personally. My consulting programming partnership was falling apart. We were also in the mini-computer business selling mini computers with our own software, and the more computers we sold the more money we lost. An associate of my partner, who had sold one of those legendary Stanford Startups for a ton of money, almost entered the business as another partner as he was looking for something new to do. Finally, after severe disagreements on business strategy, my partner and I just split up and filed lawsuits against each other. Then we both got tired of wasting money on attorneys and just quit and split, both of us taking some of the business. So then I had fewer clients and lots of time on my hands. I wrote proposals to the military services for scientific type research contracts, but also had a salesman trying to sell mini-computers to CPAs. (Certified Public Accountants) A broker who handled Paul's trading account tried to get Paul to manage money for him and his clients. Paul told him, "Go see Merk as he trades the same way I do".

That commodity broker was always looking for someone to manage commodity money as he knew he could not do it successfully himself. We talked. He introduced me to one of his clients, a Canadian from the Vancouver area in British Columbia who then was a corn hedger. He agreed to pay me $300 for a three months trial of, "The System". That was a minuscule amount of money for the project, but it forced me to become very disciplined in computing the signal numbers every day, getting formally organized, and giving the orders to buy and sell to the broker. This was about the 1st of October of 1976. The trial was to last until December 31, 1976 --- all of this for a minuscule $300.

I wanted my system to be successful so in typical engineering fashion I tested it. I had time on my hands that fall, and I devoted all my time to it. I went over all my past commodity charts. I created trading campaigns for every tradable commodity. I hand worked through each campaign, calculating the loss or gain for the last five years or so. From that I generated a distribution of results. It was a skewed normal distribution with a tail to the profit side, as you would expect from the pyramid successes. I created my own smooth function by estimation from what I could measure as the proper approximate results. I then used a random number generator to select values from this distribution function. I could then take sample input from this function that were random over the function. I then had the Stanford University Computer simulate results from a very large number (millions) of trades from this random eschewed normal distribution I had created. I had the computer do millions of simulated calculations and computed the resulting distribution of profits. I wanted a statistical confidence level of 0.50 for at least 100% profit gain per year and a statistical confidence level of 0.05 for ruin, ruin being defined as going down 50% (the client losing half his money) and, therefore, quitting. I ran calculations varying my parameters to achieve these results. I was satisfied that my system would work and produce those results. I selected as the most significant parameter, the nominal money size of the managed account, so as to give a 50% chance of gaining at least 100% per year and a 5% chance of going down 50% from any high account value.

In actual subsequent practice the System worked just like it was designed. My money raising brokers were very impressed as my system worked just like I said it would.

FOUR

COMPUTATION OF DELTA

The futures contracts that trade on the futures exchanges in the United States in their second to second trading prices are essentially random. What I mean by random is that there is no predictability. As each individual calls his or her broker and issues an order to buy and sell, these decisions made by many, many people come into the market at sundry time intervals with sundry types of orders. These events are spaced at sundry various times so that the total interaction in the markets become essentially random.

Take for example soybeans. The orders that flow into the market are placed by many different people and the effect is a price fluctuation that is essentially random. Now some might argue with this saying that obviously once a broker talks to his client and suggests a buy of soybeans and the customer agrees and places the order, then the broker calls up another customer and solicits another order, and that customer may buy also, and so on until he or she broker exhausts the list of possible prospects.

A trade house may get a huge order for beans to be delivered next December, and to protect the house from price risk may start buying futures according to some algorithm the house uses. So you might say,

"This is not random." In a certain sense, this event is not mathematically rigorously random. However, in practice the price fluctuations are more or less random, and therefore, unpredictable.

So then the question arises how can one handle the randomness to generate profit from the market?

Random events form what is called a standard distribution. A distribution is a set of events that form a pattern. For example let's take the height of the human male population of the United States. Plot the height on the horizontal axis and the number of people at that height on the vertical axes. Create little cells of the number of people at 0.001 intervals. For example people between 5.001 feet and people at 5.002 feet, and in the next cell people between 5.002 and 5.003 feet and so on. You will find as you measure these males and add up the number of people in each cell and plot the number of people in each cell that you will form what is called a normal distribution. The plot will form a curve with a rounding peak and tails that slope off to each side of the peak. The average of all the heights will be at the peak of the curve.

You will need lots of measurements to get a nice smooth curve. If you do not have enough points you may not get the smooth curve. Statisticians worry about these things and the meaning of it.

Lots of characteristics that one can measure form distributions that are "normal". For example, the intelligence quotient of a group of people also forms a "normal" distribution.

A useful calculation of a distribution is what is called standard deviation. A standard deviation is just a measurement characteristic of your distribution. Assume that the average of the distribution of male heights that you created is 5.800 feet. The standard deviation or what is called sigma (named after the Greek letter) might be 0.201 feet. This is a measure of the shape of the curve or how wide it is. It is a useful number and is talked about by statisticians when describing distributions. One can also use it to indicate where on the curve you are, for example one or two, or 3.005 standard deviations from the mean at the top of the curve and so on. For example, a 6.604 foot person night be 4.0 sigma from the mean (5.800) if sigma is 0.201.

Here is the formula for computing the standard deviation of any set of numbers.

$$\sigma_N = \left[\frac{\sum_{i=1}^{N} X_i^2 - N \sum_{i=1}^{N} X_i}{N(N-1)} \right]^{1/2}$$

Where N is the number of numbers in the set, and i is the summing variable, and X_i is the number in the set.

Now any set of numbers can be a distribution. Later in this book a number which represents the sum of all the price changes of all the futures markets will be described. It is called delta. Let's take the delta for the first trading day of July and compare it with the deltas for each trading day in the month of June. All the deltas for the month of June will form what is called a set. A set can be just a group of numbers which represent events on a possible distribution chart. All the deltas for the month of June which is a set have an average and a sigma. One can compare the delta on the first trading day of July with the set from June. How many sigma is it? This is a useful number. In practice we use small sets. We are trying to derive useful information from the market. Three day, 6 day, 9 day, 12 day, etc. sets of deltas are useful for trading purposes.

The goal in this mathematical exercise is to attempt to filter out randomness and determine price trend. Obviously, when the price of Soybeans moves from $5 to $10 over the course of several months there must be something in these events that is not random, and a price change obviously must have occurred day to day that is not random. We must somehow derive some way to filter out the randomness of the market and determine that Soybeans are going to make a price change so that we can buy before the rest of the market participants buy, and we therefore, can make a profit.

When viewed on a day to day basis, trend of prices does not much differ from randomness. Thus we must have a filter which gives some indication of trend. The indication, however, could very well be just another point of randomness. Thus we use the principals of mathematical statistics to help us, understanding that we are not being very rigorous, as we have little choice.

Therefore, one of the great tools, essentially derived from trial and error, is to compute an index of all the futures markets combined. We use a geometric index. That is, we compute an index where all the prices of all the futures contracts, the number of contracts being N, are multiplied together to form a product the n th root of which is this index. This used to be difficult before the days of computers but is more easily done now. The valuable part of this process, however, is the derivative of the index. The mathematical derivative of the index with respect to time is the sum of all the partial derivatives of the index with respect to time of each component of the index. Or in other words the delta for each day is the sum of all the changes in the amount of each future for each day divided by the price at that day. This makes it easy to compute a delta for each day, or as far as that goes, the delta for each minute, each hour, or any arbitrary period.

The basis of the usefulness of this thing is to compare each delta of each time period with a previous set. In this example use that day's delta compared with the previous set of N days. From trial and error it was found that nine days of delta for the previous period had significant meaning. Seven, eight, nine, ten, eleven, and twelve days also have meaning, but not quite as much. The meaning is that when the delta is compared with the previous nine days of delta, an event greater than 1.5 sigma indicates a high probably of change in price direction.

This becomes useful because a futures position taken on the day after a 1.5 or greater sigma day of the nine day set, has a higher probably of succeeding than a position taken on any random day. This is very useful and is an essential part of the Grand Canonical Pyramid.

FIVE

RISK CONTROL AND POSITION TAKING

In a previous Chapter we discussed delta and using the day following a greater than 1.5 sigma of delta or some other value of sigma as an entry for a position. Call a delta less than minus 1.5 a signal to buy on the following day, and a delta greater than 1.5 a signal to sell on the following day. In the following discussion we will use the examples of buying or establishing a long position. A downward market or a negative delta is used to establish a buy signal and so then to buy a long position. To establish a short position a positive delta is used as a sell signal. In all of these discussions the terms will be used in reference to a long position only. You as the reader must understand that all the terms will be reversed for establishing short positions. You will need yourself to supply the appropriate terms. We do not want to complicate this discussion by too many superfluous words.

The control of risk and the ability to make an entry into the market with a relatively low risk and low potential loss is very important, so as to have the accumulated small losses in total to be small. Here I present a set of rules to achieve that.

The rules discussed in this chapter give a significant edge for establishing positions.

Rule 5.1 ESTABLISH THE POSITION ON THE DAY WHICH FOLLOWS A SIGNAL

In practice there is no special reason that a 1.5 sigma of delta is a proper value for a signal. The 1.5 value just came from trial and error observation. Consequently, I studied the problem. I used a computer program to simulate a large number of trading entries to determine what value of sigma gave me how many signals. In the end I concluded that if I used 1.37 as a value for a trading event sigma, and require any two of the set from six days to 12 days to exceed 1.37, to give me a signal, then I obtained an average of one signal a week or one on the average for every five trading days for trading entries. This was an average over about a period of about seven years or so. I concluded that I needed a signal a week in order to be able to establish trades on a consistent basis. This computation is an inversion of a very complicated process. Computers allow one to do this as once an algorithm is conceived, one only needs to compute the outcome many, many times and obtain a distribution of results. From that distribution one can then answer the question that if I want one signal a week on the average, then what value of delta should I use to produce that. This turned out to be 1.37 for the composite calculation I was doing.

Generally, the futures position should be established on the opening of the market. When I had a large position of many contracts to establish, I would only place a few orders before the opening, since to put all my orders in the hands of the brokers before the opening tended to gun the market and result in higher prices for my trades. It is best to be circumspect about large positions. In some markets only a few score of commodity contracts can be a large position while in others it would take hundreds or even thousands of contracts to be a large trade.

Generally, the large move downward in prices that produced the signal to buy the previous day caused an amount of trepidation among bull traders so one will be essentially buying against the short-term trend. This is a real plus as when you are buying amongst a large number of sellers you will be able to establish your position quite readily.

Rule 5.2   LIQUIDATE THE POSITION ON A ½ SIGMA VIOLATION.

If the subsequent price action violates the price of the low of the day on which the signal was used to establish the position, liquidate the position.

Sigma as used in this section is the characteristic open-to-close sigma for the individual futures contract.   The computation of it was discussed previously and more discussion will be presented subsequently. This rule is to liquidate when the price of that future, for a long position, falls ½ sigma below the low of the day on which the position was established. This is an intraday rule, that is, any time the price falls below the get out point, the position is liquidated immediately.   Some use resting stop orders. I have always been paranoid about locals on the trading floor looking over the shoulder of the broker with the stop deck and seeing my order, so I seldom used open stop orders, but had my trading screen or my brokers screen set to beep when the price fell below the get out point. I then would, subsequently, just place a market order with the brokerage firms who handled my positions. I don't think this cost me anything and in fact probably saved my clients lots of money as often my stop point was right where lots of other traders had their stop points, so the market would run through this stop point rapidly, drop below it and rally once the locals got through running the stops and were covering their short positions.   My sell orders would then pile in a few minutes or so afterwards and then be executed while the locals were usually buying and covering their short positions in a price rally.

This ½ sigma rule is required in order to keep losses small. I never conducted a detailed study as to whether a slightly different amount than ½ sigma would be better or worse. I never would have believed that it would have made any difference, as one must have a get out rule to keep losses small. It must be placed somewhere and where one places it is completely random and the result would also be random anyway. The closer the stop point is the more likely it is to be executed. The farther away the stop point is the larger will be the loss when the trade losses. When one compares the amount of the loss and the frequency of losses, I found that a ½ sigma kept my loss rate to about 50 %. That is, half of my trade entries resulted in losses because of the ½ sigma rule   The loss rate over a long period of time because of this rule and other get out rules resulted in an overall loss rate of 62%. In my overall trading over a more than 10 year period, 62% were small losers, 33% were small profits, and 5% of all trades were big gainers which produced profits much greater than all the accumulated small losses.

These numbers are not much different than that for a batting average for a baseball player. There may be something really fundamental here. It seems the game of baseball was designed to produce such success rates also. As a trader what I was looking for was a gofer ball down the middle of the plate that I could hit out of the park. That occurred in about 5% of my trades.

One uses as a sigma for a particular future contract the characteristic sigma. By that I mean the sigma that the future has generated for the last few months or so maybe up to a year of the past. I passed an N day square convolution function over the data and computed the difference between the open and close prices. From this set of open to close differences the sigma is computed. A problem occurs when, as sometimes happens, a bull move is happening and the sigma starts to increase. An increasing sigma is usually a very bullish sign. The market, "wakes up", so to speak because of some fundamental that the bull traders are discovering, and they are starting to play in the market. Others don't believe it and start to play by selling. This causes greater up and down price activity in the market and creates greater volatility and so increases the sigma. When this happens one must increase the characteristic sigma one uses for the futures contract. In practice we used a six-week convolution to determine the new sigma. You must be very careful here. If you increase the sigma too quick you will destroy the potential of a rapid pyramid and great profits. On the other hand, using too small a sigma results in considerable increased risk, and the potential for a huge loss when you have a large position. Some of the worst disasters are caused by a large increase in sigma (volatility) and the subsequent huge price move against your position when you have pyramided into a large position using a small sigma.

Rule 5.3   LIQUIDATE THE POSITION ON A VIOLATION OF ANY SUBSEQUENT SIGNAL TWO DAYS ON THE CLOSE.

Once a position has been established and the market moves up and the signal used to establish the position has not been violated, a new buy signal will happen. This will give you a new get out price above the get out price established on the entry signal. Once you are in a profit in that position you should try to keep that position going as long as possible until it is clearly established that the trend is not continuing. Thus use a two-day rule. On the day following that of the new signal use the low of that day as a get out point, but only on the second day violation. However, use it only during the closing range. For practical reasons, however, you must decide about 5 minutes before the close if the market is going to close below your stop point as few exchanges now take stop close only orders. As soon as you decide that the market is going to close below the get out point put in market orders to liquidate.

Rule 5.4   **LIQUIDATE THE POSITION INTRADAY WHEN THE PRICE MOVES DOWN THREE SIGMA BELOW A HIGH CLOSE WHICH OCCURRED DURING THE LAST THREE WEEKS.**

This is a failsafe out and applies to all the positions all the time. Normally, this rule doesn't occur when establishing positions because the price is too far below the market. However, you must always have this place on your chart (or in your computer) as the place you will always liquidate. Sometimes when you create a position after a sell off on a buy signal the market may be near this THREE sigma get out point. This often is a very good entry as it gets you in at low prices. However, this future's overall price up move may be about to end, and your get in timing is just before a market collapse which now is going to cost you. Have this point on your chart as well as your ½ sigma point. These are places where you liquidate without thinking about it. You must control risk and save your money for the next opportunity.

RISK CONTROL AND POSITION TAKING

SIX

STRUCTURE

Structure is the art of trade selection. In this Chapter you will be given the rules whereby you select what future to trade.

What you are looking for is a futures contract which has the potential for a big move, that is, a big change in price, probably in the next few weeks. Before a clear trend gets started it is impossible to distinguish between a random event which looks like a potential move and an event which looks the same but will result in a substantial move.

The best mental outlook is to have an attitude to trade as little as possible. Only take a trade when these rules say you must. It is certainly best not to overtrade. You are like a baseball player waiting for a gofer ball down the middle of the plate at a perfect height. When the ball just leaves the pitchers hand it may look good but it's hard to tell the spin on the ball and where it exactly is going to cross the plate.

Good potential trades have high absolute volatility. Dead markets with no volatility do not go anywhere. Markets with no trend do not go anywhere. Trend is the slope of the price curve. A good way to measure the opportunity of a trend is tau multiplied by lambda divided by 2.0 sigma. What is this? Tau is the slope of the basic trend line on the chart of the futures contract in dollars (or any other measure such as ticks, cents, pounds, etc) per day. Lambda is the average time period between signals or since you are using signals on the average five days apart, lambda is 5.0 days. Sigma is the characteristic standard deviation of the future's price volatility in the same units that you measured tau. This trend potential opportunity determining ratio should be between 1.0 and 2.0. If the ratio is near one or below, the future is just going up and down and is going nowhere, so avoid it. If the ratio is near 2.0 or above then there is not enough volatility to support the trend, or in other words the traders in the market are not testing the market by up and down extremes. So to take a trade in this future then is very high risk as it is subject to sharp price reversals and, therefore, is to be avoided.

Rule 6.1 A FUTURES BUY MUST HAVE THREE WEEKS IN TREND.

A long position must have an upward trend for at least three weeks. Watch for futures which suddenly wake up and start a trend. Somebody knows something and is accumulating. When this goes on for three weeks it is time to get involved.

Rule 6.2 A FUTURES BUY MUST HAVE TWO BUY SIGNALS NOT VIOLATED.

What we are looking for is good structure. Good structure has the sell signals violated and the buy signals holding, that is, not violated. Put the signal arrows on your price chart. You will soon see which futures contracts are a potential trade.

Rule 6.3   BUY ON THE THIRD BUY SIGNAL WHEN THE FUTURE IS IN A TREND.

As soon as you see an upward trend with the right tau*lambda/2*sigma with two buy signals already holding, buy it on the next buy signal

All of these rules have their short side counterpart. It would be confusing in this write up to always express the wording for shorts and longs in the same writing. Thus you, the reader, must substitute the correct verbiage for a short trade. All the rules are the same. There is no absolute difference between long and short trades. Generally, however, for really big moves, the long side has more potential, because there is no limit to how high a futures can go while in a short trade the futures can only go as far as zero.

SEVEN

BUYING IN THE PYRAMID

We have discussed trade entry and low loss trade exit in previous Chapters. Here we will discuss how to conduct the Grand Canonical Pyramid, herein otherwise known as the GCP.

You have established a position. You have bought N contracts. In order for the pyramid calculations to be relatively smooth you should have five contracts to start with. The minimum must be at least three contracts in order to have any semblance of a pyramid.

You have calculated a characteristic sigma for the futures contract as discussed on the chapter on risk. The money you should have behind this position should be at least three sigma per contract. So for a five contract position you will have 15 sigma behind this position. Generally, three sigma is around the minimum margin sum requirement of the brokerage firm. Sometimes when the regulators or the broker firms get nervous they will raise the margin requirements above these amounts. You should take that as an indication that the regulators and/or brokers potentially are going to interfere in this market and do weird things. Thus you would be well advised to not trade this market and wait for another opportunity in some other future.

You have established your position. You have not been stopped out and the position shows a profit. As your profits increase you will buy on the close additional contracts every time another seven sigma of profit has been generated. So if you started with five contracts or 15 sigma in dollars in your account, when your account gets to 22 sigma you will add another contract on the close only. Now you have six contracts. As the price moves up on six contracts and another seven sigma of profit is generated you will add another contract. You will add as many contracts as you can on the close every day that the market moves up to where you have an additional seven sigma of profit for each contract you add, according to the following rules.

Rule 7.1 ADD ONLY WHEN THE PRICE IS IN THE CLEAR

Do not add when a sell signal is over the market. You have been adding contracts on the close as the price moves up. You compute a sell signal. You must stop pyramiding until the price has moved through that sell signal for two days on the close. Thus you must wait until the second day on the close that the price has moved through the price level of the signal before you add more contracts.

Rule 7.2 ADD ON BUY SIGNALS

As the market moves up and down and you have been waiting for the price to get into the clear (that is above all sell signals) so that you can add more contracts, you may get another buy signal. This is an opportunity to also add to your position. Buy on the opening or soon after on the day after the buy signal was generated. The number of contracts you will buy is computed on the basis of your fail safe get out point. Your fail-safe get out point is an intraday point three sigma below the highest close. This acts like the ½ sigma liquidation point rule. When the price goes through that point everything is liquidated immediately.

Compute how much profit you have left if you had to get out at the three sigma point. Assume you get out at that point and have left seven sigma in profit. Therefore, you can add one contract on the opening on the day after the buy signal generation. You need to give yourself a little room here. If the present price is considerably above the get out price you will also need to take that into account, because the contract that you buy will also lose money at the fail safe get out point. Thus perhaps you may need 8 to 9 sigma to add a contract when the price is far away from the fail safe get out point.

Add aggressively as often as you can and as many as you can. This is what produces spectacular profits. However, never add new money to this pyramid. That is asking for disaster. Only add on the basis of profits. On the other hand, at the first sign that something is seriously wrong, liquidate.

Rule 7.3   STOP ALL PYRAMIDING AFTER A GAP GREATER THAN ½ SIGMA.

A gap is a move on your price chart where the high of the previous day is below the low of the present day under consideration. That gap should be greater than ½ sigma for this rule to take effect. Sometimes the market will open up with a gap but will fill the gap in as the day progresses. This is fine. Often old pro traders will sell against their large positions on the opening with the strategy of buying back on the close to support their position. If the gap is not filled during the day the shorts are getting trapped and this injects technical structural weakness into the market and increases the risk. Therefore, with an unfilled gap you do not add any more on the close.

Rule 7.4   STOP ALL PYRAMIDING AFTER AN UP LIMIT MOVE

The exchanges set arbitrary limits on how far the price can move from the previous days close. This is really dumb and unfortunate for it interferes with free flowing market action. But the underlying motive for this is that since futures contracts are marked to the market every day (settlement occurs and your account is credited or debited every day the amount of profit or loss your positions have generated that day) this protects the brokerage firm in that it gives them time to call you up to get margin money out of you. As the price moves down limit for example and your position generates a margin call, they will want you to meet that call immediately. If the next day the price goes down limit again, they will again demand you meet another margin call. If this were to ever happen to you, however, and you think you are trapped and cannot get out, don't believe it, as you can always do a switch to the nearby contract and sell it (since it usually does not have limits) or offset your position in the cash markets.

Rule 7.5   LOAD UP ON BUY SIGNALS

If for any reason you have sold part or all of your position and are waiting for developments, buy all you can on a buy signal using seven sigma of profit for each contract you add to your base position. Your initial base position only needs three sigma behind each contract. Your base position is the number of contracts you initially started your campaigns with. It should be five or more contracts, but if you do not want to risk that much money it can be as low as three contracts. For less than three you cannot really effectively pyramid.

BUYING IN THE PYRAMID

EIGHT

SELLING THE PYRAMID

Let's now assume you have been pyramiding a position and you have a substantial profit. It is very important to be very careful as you are assuming great risk. Remember the old college frat dictum, "He who hesitates is lost".

Rule 8.1   **SELL YOUR WHOLE POSITION ON ANY VIOLATION OF ANY BUY SIGNAL TWO DAYS ON THE CLOSE.**

You have been adding to your position and you get a buy signal and load up. If the price moves against you and violates this buy signal or any previous buy signal, liquidate everything on the second day of violation of that signal on the close.

Rule 8.2   **SELL ½ THE POSITION ON THE FIRST LOWER CLOSE GREATER THAN ½ SIGMA AFTER A GAP GREATER THAN ½ SIGMA**

Your future is moving up nicely. You have a gap in the price action that is greater than ½ sigma. The market may continue to move up and keep making more gaps. In fact this is just exactly what you have been waiting for and it is making you lots of money. The risk is now getting greater and it is time to think about taking profits. The first day the market closes lower by an amount greater than ½ sigma from the previous close, sell half the position.

Rule 8.3 SELL ½ THE POSITION ON THE NEXT SELL SIGNAL AFTER A GAP GREATER THAN ½ SIGMA

Again your futures is moving up nicely. You have had a gap greater than ½ sigma so that you are not adding any more. You get a sell signal. Sell ½ your position on the opening or soon after.

Rule 8.4 THE QUEUE RULE

This is a complicated rule but it is very, very important. This is the one rule that will make you a lot of money. You compute three sigma multiplied by the square root of N, where N is the number of days to a previous close. This is a running calculation and must be done every day when you have a pyramided position. When the price reaches intraday the price level you compute using this rule you will liquidate ¼ the position. For example, you have computed your three sigma. If the price intraday exceeds the price from the previous days close by three sigma, you will sell ¼ of your position. (This is three sigma multiplied by the square root of 1.0 which is 1.0.) You will do this with a resting order to sell at that price, or if you have a large position sell at the market as soon as your screen beeper (or your brokers screen) hits that price.

If the price level intraday exceeds the price at the close two days ago by three sigma multiplied by the square root of 2.0 (1.414) then sell ¼ the position. Sell only once during the day. If the price exceeds both the one day and two day price you will have a chance to sell another ¼ the next day. If the price level intraday exceeds the price at the close three days ago by three sigma multiplied by the square root of 3.0 (1.732) then sell ¼ the position. Compute these numbers out to seven. Generally, very few markets touch the seven day rule or any greater number without setting off a smaller number. When you have a pyramided position, compute these get out numbers all the way up to seven days every day. Often you will find the seven get out prices are sort of grouped together. When the price gets there sell the ¼. The next day repeat the process. The most successful campaigns I have ever conducted ended with this selling rule. I once sold thousands of contracts of Gold for my clients at $860 per once (the highest it ever got was $864 and never exceeded that high again for the next 30 years) according to this rule making them millions of dollars. Other really great campaigns also ended with this rule. It does not happen very often. If you are able to liquidate all of your position with this rule by selling on four days in a row ¼ of the position, it is OVER. I mean OVER! Forget about this market, go home and buy your wife or significant other some jewels, (If you have a husband, I am not sure what you would buy him, maybe a safari trip to Africa to hunt lions), and quit and take a well-deserved rest. Taking risks like this is addictive, especially if you have made a lot of money. Have enough sense to hang it up for a while and let your money dry out, and let your inner self take real possession of your money. It is funny money only as long as you let it be funny money.

NINE

THE GRAND CANONICAL PYRAMID

What you are trying to achieve is an exponential growth in trading profits through a trading campaign. The secret here is to lose money linearly but make money exponentially. As we discussed in a previous chapter it is the 5% of the trades that have the potential for a large profit and those you will try to trade exponentially. You do not want to miss any of them. If you trade all year taking your losses faithfully and then miss out on the one really big move for the year you have failed. Generally, there is at least one really big move each year. You job is to identify it, get aboard and go for it with all the skill you have. You cannot know ahead of time which trade will be the gofer ball in the middle of the plate. Therefore, you must take every clear opportunity. Take your losses and keep them small. Do not fight the markets but wait patiently for the right trade. I once took 13 losses in a row. One of my clients said to me, "Even my eight year old could do better than that". He was right. It takes real skill to lose 13 times in a row.

Here is the fundamental formula for pyramid success:

$$\$ = bN \left(e^{a(P-P_0)} - 1 \right)/a$$

Where $\$$ is the dollars gained
$P - P_0$ is the overall price change of the future
a is the factor used to add contracts, in our case 1/7s

59

s is the standard deviation, the characteristic sigma of the future
b is the relationship between dollars and price

$$\text{where } (d\$) = bN(dp)$$

where small d stands for the difference or little delta

N_0 = the number of starting contracts

If the dollars gained is reduced to the number of sigma's of profit and we use 7s as the add requirement sum then the formula becomes:

$$\$ = 7sN_0 \left(e^{(P - P_0)/7s} - 1 \right)$$

The important part of the formula to look at is the exponent of the e. e is the natural logarithm base and has a value of 2.7183. e to the 2.0 power is a little over 7, e to the 3rd power is about 20, e to the 4th power is about 55, e to the 5th 150, e 6th 400, e 7th 1000, e 8th 3000, e 9th 8000, and e 10th 20,000. This is a gross estimate of the ratio of your starting money to the money you may have at the end of the campaign. What you want is the campaign where you achieve 100 times your original start money or more.

Take for example soybeans. Assume a sigma of twenty cents or $1000 a contract. Seven sigma is $1.40 or $7,000 per contract. Assume a seven dollar move, from $12 beans to $19 in beans over about a ten week period. The seven dollar move divided by the seven sigma of $1.40 is about five. e to the 5th power is about 150. Thus potentially, a 150 to 1 return on your original starting capital is possible for a $7 move in beans when you have a sigma of about twenty cents. If you started with five contracts or 25,000 bushels of beans or about $15,000 in minimum margin requirements (given the exchange minimum margin requirement is about $3,000 for a five thousand bushel contract) you could end up with about $5,000,000 for a successful campaign. The formula above indicates you started with $7sN_0$ or $7,000 times an

N_0 of five or \$35,000. \$35,000 times 150 is about \$5,000,000. Of course, remember the old adage, there is many a slip between the cup and the lip. In actual practice you could start with anything above the exchange minimum margin. So in this example the original \$15,000 at exchange minimum became five million dollars, given you were able to stay with the position for the whole seven dollar move.

Now, of course, it is not all that easy. The potential is there. It will take courage, discipline, and a little luck. Sometimes regulators influenced by politicians, or exchanges get in the way and make arbitrary changes in the trading rules. This can be a potential for a real disaster. You must keep your wits about you at all times. You must keep your thinking clear at all times. Carefully make the calculations described in this book every day. Do not let yourself get distracted. Do not let your emotions get involved. You must have nerves of steel. When your clear thinking mind observes, and the calculations indicate that the campaign is over, get out, take a rest, and let your money dry out.

My clients once had a huge position in soybeans, wheat, and corn in the summer of 1988. The campaign had been going on for eight weeks or so. Indications were the end was near. This severe drought of 1988 in the Corn Belt was making nightly news. Churches all over were praying for rain. On a Friday I started to liquidate. I was trading on west coast time and beans close at 11:15 am   Beans were still going up and I got involved in a long telephone call mid-morning with one of my best money raising brokers. The television monitors were all talking about the drought and the predictions of the weather people was that the week end was to be very hot and dry all over the mid-west. I allowed myself to get distracted and only liquidated about 20% of the position. Needless to say, a freak, "backdoor", weather system (which was apparently predicted by the European model weather computer which few people paid any attention too) dumped three inches of rain on Iowa and Illinois on Saturday. Soybeans were then down limit three days in a row with no trading and my clients lost a good share of their profits. Don't let those kinds of things happen to you. This is a game of mathematics and statistics. Play by the rules no matter what is happening or what the news is. The markets anticipate news. When the news happens, it is over.

To make the $100,000,000, (one hundred million dollars) the amount projected by this book, the overall strategy is to participate in three e to the 4th power moves. 4th power moves occur fairly often. A 4th power move is about a 50:1 return. If you keep on the average 30:1 on three moves you will have a 20,000 to 1 return which should allow you to keep 10,000 to 1. So if you start with $10,000 and make three 30:1 campaigns, you can expect to keep maybe $100,000,000.

Most markets are not big enough and liquid enough to handle a $100,000,000 end game. Therefore, the candidate for your last 30:1 campaign has to be in a future that has huge open interest and liquidity. The primary candidates would be crude oil, gold, or interest rates. Interest rates, however, can be very dangerous because the government can and does manipulate them. Just when your campaign seems about to succeed some government spokesman can make an announcement, or make some arbitrary decision, and your position can turn sour without any warning or with any mathematical or statistical indication. So be careful when trading interest rates.

THE GOLD CAMPAIGN OF 1980

As an example of a very successful pyramid campaign consider The Gold Play of 1979 -1980. The actual charts used in the campaign are on pages 64 and 66. Note that the charts roll over when going off the top of the page and continue on to the bottom of the page, sometimes with a change of scale with the indicated prices just to the left of the plotted daily price action. The March 1980 contract is in blue and the September contract is in purple. The buy and sell signals are in red. On the second chart on page 66 the December contract is in red and the June contract is in green with the buy and sell signals in blue.

Briefly, note that the gold price move consolidated in October, and a position was initiated November 14, 1979 at a price in the March contract of about $410 per ounce. The client base put us into about 200 IMM Gold contracts of 100 oz. each. After a week or so the price gaped up. The buy signal on Dec 7th enabled a large addition to the position. There is a one week consolidation in the first part of December and then the price breaks out and really starts to move. We continually added to the clients positions as the price moved up right through the Christmas holidays. We loaded up on the buy signal on 12/28/79. A gap occurred so pyramiding was stopped after New Years Day. A buy signal was generated on 1/10/80 so we again loaded up at about $615. At that point we had about 1500 contracts. The market gapped away so pyramiding was stopped. The queue rule went into effect about 1/16/80. A sell signal was generated 1/18/80. With that sell signal, gaps, and the queue rule, the position was completely liquidated by 1/21/80 at averages prices of about $860.

1500 contracts at a price of about $860 is about 130 million dollars' worth of gold. The clients made millions of dollars on this one campaign. The time this campaign took was about ten weeks. You can do it too. All it takes is discipline, patience to wait for the opportunity, and courage.

We encouraged clients to remove their profits as we traded a fixed portfolio size. One of my clients bought a hot zorch automobile with some of his profits. He added custom license plates with the letters IMMGOLD. We had done most of our trading on the Chicago IMM futures market.

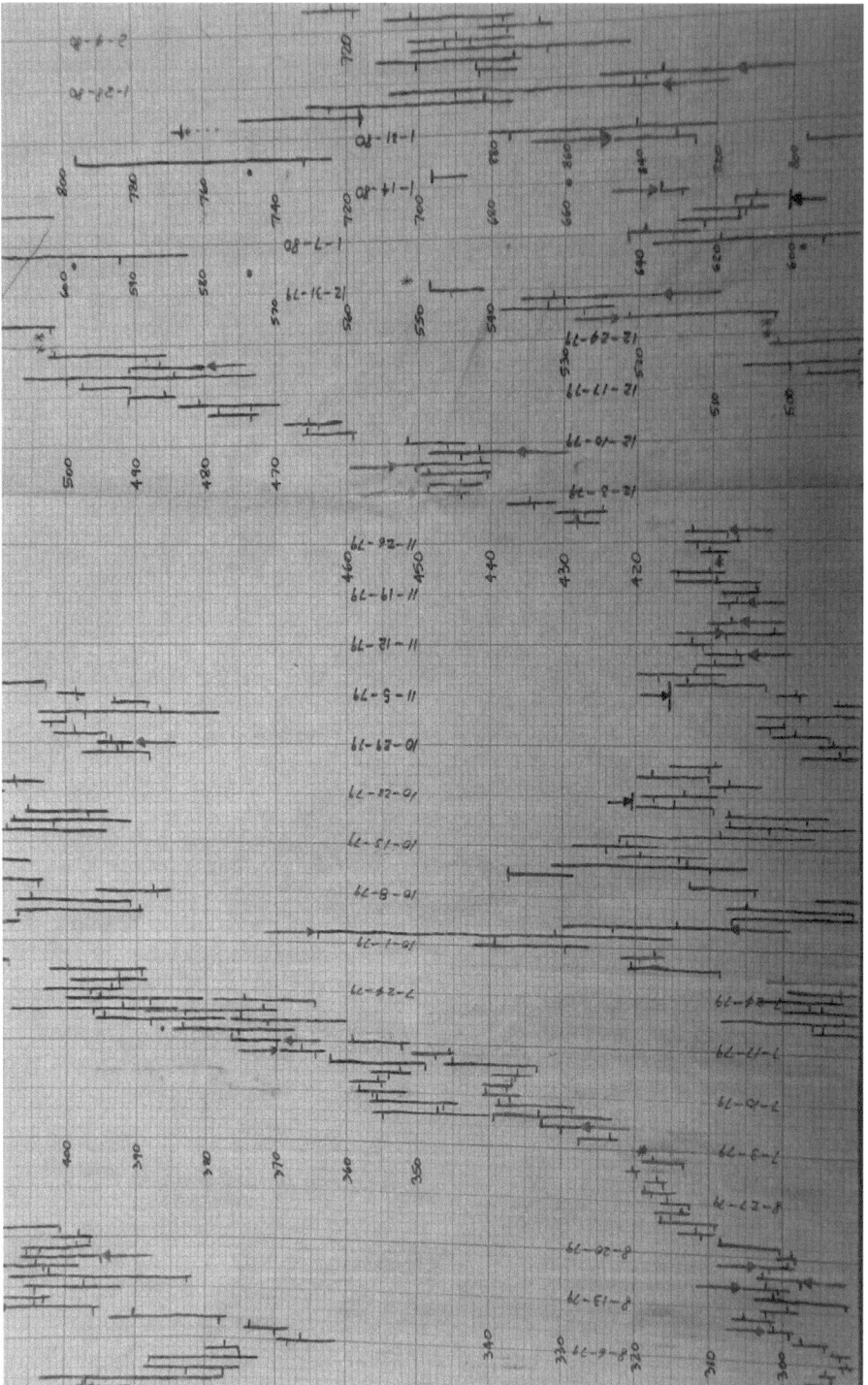

Apparently this gold market action was related to the Iran Hostage Crisis where United States diplomats and employees were taken hostage by Iranians on November 4, 1979. Ten days later the clients position in gold was established. The up move was technical and not related to any real shortage of gold. Knowledge of the planning for a rescue operation by the US military was probably leaked into the rumor mills, and this caused the top in the gold bubble on January 21, 1980.

This is why you will play technically using a statistical approach. The price is everything and it seems impossible to really know the real fundamentals of supply and demand in any market, or what is going on in the rumor and leak conundrum. The number of participants is vast and their individual motivations unknowable.

I suggest in this quest to become rich you maintain and plot your own charts. This will give you a clearer understanding of what is going on. I plotted all my charts using nearly the same relative scale. The gold charts on pages 64 and 66 are a good example of my style of charting. Note that the price range from the bottom of the chart to the stop of the chart is approximately an increase of 20% to 33% over the price at the bottom of the chart. When using something like this as a proximate scale for all of your charts, the amount of volatility in the price variation is more obvious. Volatile price action is what makes money. If the volatility is obvious, one is more likely to participate.

Sometimes this style makes the chart harder to read for subsequent observers as you can see from the crushed plotting representing what happened in the final blowout stage of the gold bubble. It also makes the bubble more obvious as in the final stages of the gold move the daily price plotted went from the bottom of the cart to the top of the chart several times rather quickly in less than a week. It reflected a huge percentage change in the price of gold.

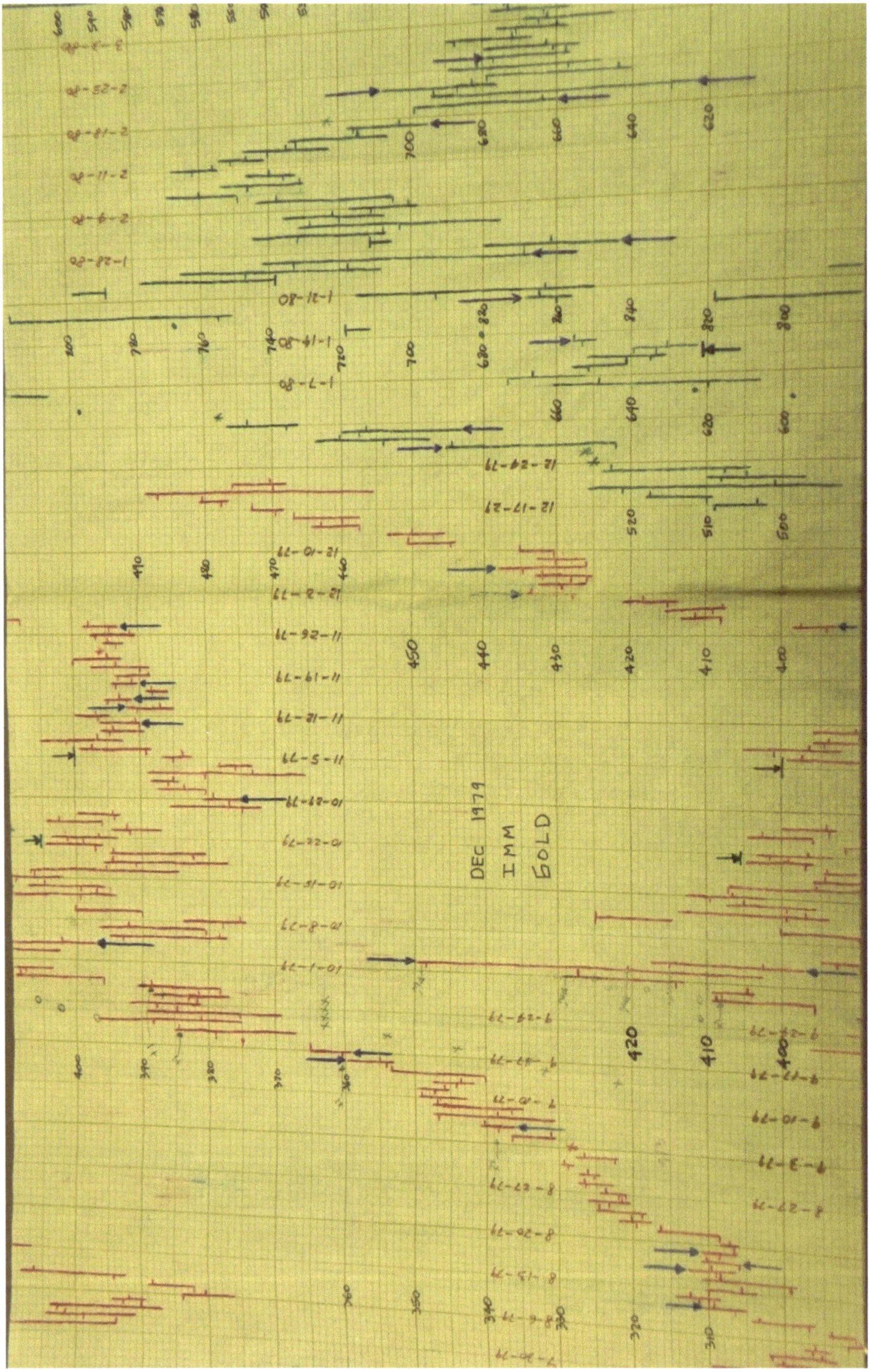
DEC 1979
IMM
GOLD

That gold market was indeed a fantastic oportunity to make a lot of money. Markets like that will come again. You must be ready and prepared.

TEN

THE SIX DRAGONS

If you would climb Everest, which is the epitome of the mountain climbing experience, which is really of the same psychological experience as the Grand Canonical Pyramid, which you are going to attempt; then it is required that you apply the same quality and quantity of effort. To succeed you will require all the resources of mind, body, and spirit you can generate. Let's call this futures climbing Everest project the Grand Canonical Pyramid. (GCP) In order to succeed you must slay six dragons of emotion. This is not easy. It takes all the self-discipline, mental and psychological resources you can muster. Yet you must conquer and slay these dragons with no pity. These six dragons are FEAR, GREED, PRIDE, ATTACHMENT (falling in love with a position), EUPHORIA, GUILT.

Why do I can them dragons? They are sort of mystical, that is they have a spiritual dimension, somewhat difficult to rationally define, and differ in how they operate within each individual person. They are very difficult to fight, and it is not clear how they are to be fought. Yet, slay these dragons you must. They are:

FEAR

Fear is the emotion of being afraid. You look into the abyss and you get the shakes. When I was a child living in rural Wisconsin my father took me one day to the big city of Winona across the Mississippi River in Minnesota. I remember going over a very high rickety bridge. My mother loved to shop and wander around in cities. So to maybe kill some time my father took me to the top of a high skyscraper (at least for Winona) to see the view. When I looked over the edge I became petrified. I was just immobilized by fear. I never forgot it. So you too when you consider risking your money, maybe hard earned money, that you really would rather keep, you can be seized with the fear of losing it.

This getting rich campaign is a business of mathematics, statistics, and rational analysis. Emotions like fear cannot and must not enter into it. Emotions must be suppressed and eliminated from your soul, and not have any influence on your mind in its thinking. You cannot and must not have any emotion or psychological attachment in this awesome quest to become really rich.

Emotions will make you make decisions that will defeat your purpose which is to create money out of nothing. In your quest you must develop nerves of steel. You are to become an ice man, like what it takes to become a combat fighter pilot where your mission is to kill the enemy without mercy, and if you do not kill, you will be killed yourself. You are fearless and you will make and suffer the six g turns to gain the advantage over your opponent and you will not even think about the consequences of it. So it is with the successful commodity futures speculator going after the big win. You go for it with everything you have using only rational analysis. The great Chinese General, Sun Tzu, of about 300 BC or so said, and I paraphrase it a bit as it is in Chinese,

"What is called, 'foreknowledge', cannot be elicited from spirits, nor from gods, nor by analogy with past events, nor from calculations. It must be obtained from men who know the enemy situation".

Thus know yourself, and know that you, yourself, no less are the enemy. In the immortal words of the comic character Pogo, "We have met the enemy and he is us'". Also know that understanding another enemy, in this case, understanding the market operation, and that the application of mathematical statistics to the markets, wins, not clairvoyance.

GREED

Greed as said by my ole mentor, Paul, is expecting to get more out of a situation than one can rationally expect. You can be seized by greed. You want it so you pursue it and take it. Greed is a very subtle thing. Sometimes it is very hard to identify. Most people condemn greed and think most large corporations and even ordinary business men as greedy. That kind of greed, if it is really greed, is not what I am talking about. We traders and speculators all seek to gain, and that is not greed. Gain is very normal and part of ordinary life. But it can come to the point where the desire for the gain of something overwhelms and exceeds what one can rationally expect. This is the kind if greed I am talking about.

Greed as an emotion can destroy your rational thinking and cause you to make great errors. At all times keep your wits about you and rationally analyze what is going on and not try to get something out of something else what is really not there. Greed is devastating and can destroy your quest for the GCP.

PRIDE

You can easily become proud of yourself. After a few successes you may start to think to yourself, "I am really starting to make this work". Nothing is farther from the truth. You will never understand this thing. This is a game of mathematics and statistics. It is similar but not the same as a gaming casino. Sometimes you win, sometimes you lose. You will never do it right. If you start to think of yourself as able and lucky and smart and qualified to do this thing you will be proven wrong. You are nothing but a hound dog on the trail of the great GCP. You are nothing. Do not think highly of yourself; it will lead to great error and loss of much money.

ATTACHMENT, FALLING IN LOVE

It is easy to fall in love with your futures position or a particular futures contract. You have been making money in soybeans. You start to love soybeans. They make you nice money because the price goes up and down in a nice orderly set of sequences. So on beans you place your affection and love and become attached. Your rationality is now destroyed and you will lose lots of money and miss opportunities.

It is like the really cute siren you were infatuated with in high school. You did everything you could to get her attention and get her for a date. The infatuation consumed you. Well if that happens to you in the futures markets, you are dead, finished.

Do not fall in love with any position. Again, this is a game of mathematics and statistics. Rational analysis must prevail. Beans, corn, gold, or anything else is the mechanism through which you will create money out of nothing and become rich. You do not love them or place your affection on them. There is nothing intrinsically good or cute about any commodity or futures contract.

It is very important not to tell anybody about your position when you are in the middle of a campaign. This is especially true of your wife or significant other. Talking to someone about your position establishes ownership of the position in your mind. That is the last thing you want. Your position is the mechanism that is going to make you rich. You do not own it so tell no one about it. You can create an illusion in your mind that it is yours, and so you try to protect it and keep it. This is disaster. Again, this is a game of mathematics and statistics. Do not get attached to any position. You must be able to quickly liquidate it when the time and opportunity comes.

EUPHORIA

When this thing really starts to work and you create huge quantities of notional money along comes that great joy of big success called euphoria. Your spirit ascends to the heavens. Your exuberance knows no bounds. You may even leap for joy and start to celebrate like a winning football team. If this happens to you before you have moved your money into a nice safe bank, you are dead, finished. Your rational analysis thinking is now so clouded that you will not be able to see disaster approach. Euphoria is a terrible emotion when the game is not yet over, and will cause you to make terrible errors. Again, you must keep your wits about you and keep your mind clear. This is a game of mathematics and statistics. It is not over till it is over. To have euphoria before you have safely stored your money away in a long term untouchable place (even perhaps like land or buried gold), destroys your ability to make rational decisions, and you will lose all that money for sure.

GUILT

This is an emotion almost nobody ever expects to have when trying to achieve great success. If it comes to the point in your campaign to conquer the GCP, when you feel guilty about making so much money you are finished, done for. Your capability for making rational mathematical and statistical decisions that are correct is over. Feeling guilty about making so much money destroys your ability to trade profitably. I know it is hard to believe, but I have been there. It is verily true.

Now it is important and correct to feel guilty when you have done something wrong. It leads to repentance. Correctly living a clean moral life is a great asset to your effort to become rich. It is important to not be distracted by sundry problems and emotions, which arrive from immoral living, or taking advantage of sundry people and institutions. If you have to watch out for cops, the IRS, an ex, enforcers, or sundry enemies appearing on your back trail, you will not be able to devote your full undivided attention to achieving the great GCP.

As a summary to this emotion discombobulating, let's consider some more very thoughtful words from the famous Chinese general, Sun Tzu. The General in his culture was the man who directed the activities of the army. You too are the General in charge of climbing up the great Grand Canonical Pyramid.

FIVE POOR QUALITIES IN A GENERAL

RECKLESS/KILLED A general who is stupid and courageous is a calamity. Courage is just one quality. A valiant general will be certain to enter an engagement recklessly, and if so will not appreciate what is advantageous.

COWARDLY/CAPTURED One who esteems life above all will be overcome with hesitancy. Hesitancy is a great calamity,

QUICK-TEMPERED/FOOL An impulsive man can be provoked to rage and brought to death. One easily angered is irascible, obstinate, and hasty. He does not consider difficulties.

PRIDE, SENSE OF HONOR/CALLUMNIATE One anxious to defend his reputation pays no regard to anything else.

COMPASSIONATE/HARASS One who fears causalities cannot give up temporary advantage for a long-term gain, and is unable to let go to seize it.

THE RUIN OF THE ARMY AND THE DEATH OF THE GENERAL ARE THE INEVITABLE RESULTS OF THESE SHORT COMINGS.

So end the words of Sun Tzu.

ELEVEN

MISSCELLANEOUS CONSIDERATIONS

GENERAL THINGS

Do not get emotionally involved with any position. This is a business of mathematics and statistics. Success occurs only with patience and fortitude in rule following.

Do not cheer, hope, and pray for price increase or decrease. Liquidate under such situations when you have reached the point of praying, hoping, or cheering. Success comes from rule following rather than changes in prices.

You must be involved in every potential opportunity, therefore, do not take risks that result in unavailability or destruction of your funds because when opportunity does arrive you must have funds.

Liquidate on the rules. Liquidate when they close the exchange, have record volume, or national news media is talking and writing about the price of the commodity or futures instrument, etc., etc. Do not hope, wish, or wait for higher prices when such events occur. National news means it is soon to be over.

Greed is your biggest enemy. When rules are violated in hope of higher gain you are a victim of greed. Greed is a desire to make more out of a situation than you can rationally expect.

You must be in every active future that has a good trend and a good tau*lamda/2.0*sigma. (Between 1.0 and 2.0) If not, establish a position on the next signal.

On large corrections, liquidate correlated futures. For example, if gold breaks, liquidate long silver, if correlated. Be careful here. This must be done with rational analysis.

Sometimes the rules do not work. Stand aside and wait for new opportunity. One must plan to lose 65% of the time.

The most overriding criterion, that which leads to the greatest success, is to stay with a good position. A good position has good trend, good volatility, good structure, and good tau*lamda/2.0*sigma. (Between 1.0 and 2.0) Stay with such positions until evidence to the contrary. Do not be tempted to take premature profits.

Do not guess tops and bottoms. It does not work. Do not panic or fix on your fears. Remember: Capital, Discipline, Courage.

Read your emotions. Fear leads to poor liquidation, greed to disaster, euphoria and guilt to very muddled thinking. Do not act on the basis of emotions, but read these emotions and compensate.

This is statistical system. It loses most of the time. 63% of the trades lose and only one trade in twenty makes any substantial money. Remember that in throwing a pair of dice, snake eyes occurs on the average once in every 36 throws. You are like the baseball player batting 320. You get on base less than a third of the times at bat.

Survival is the most important criterion to optimize in any situation. Patience is the supreme virtue. One must still be around when the right situation presents itself.

At all times you will stay relaxed, looking for opportunity. It is very important not to force any situation. Once something really starts to go, however, then really concentrate on the big push, but do not get attached to it so that you cannot liquidate when the technical situation dictates a retreat.

SOME TACTICAL RULES TO IMPROVE PERFORMANCE

When you have a large position, tape read around the sig/2 point. Be quick once sig/2 is broken significantly. Keep small new lows.

Liquidate on the close with violation on the close after two to five day distribution or sideways move. This can be less than ½ sigma after distribution. Use at least ½ sigma when there is no distribution.

You must liquidate on a two day violation on the close. In a large pyramid if the violation is slight, keep ½ of the position. Liquidate the remainder if no quick reversal of the violation.

Liquidate ½ the position on a trend line violation. (Trend line violation greater than ½ sigma) Draw trend lines on 1st, 2nd, 3rd, sets of lows. Liquidate on significant violations especially on close. Watch for distributions which violate trend lines. Liquidate on large price change or key reversal.

On contract roll overs when you move your position by a switch from one futures month to the next, liquidate half of the position, especially in hogs or cattle.

In a pyramid liquidate on nine day relative trend reversal, that is, the relative trend is less than the market trend.

Liquidate on the next lower close after a large change in price in a distribution phase. Do this especially after sloppy structure or lowering relative trend.

In a pyramid liquidate on a false breakout reversal. This can be one, two, three, or four days. You must have good reasons to stay with the position, such as especially good fundamentals or real good relative trend. You liquidate on poor relative trend, large downward price change, or other indication of weakness.

You liquidate when contrary sell signals consecutively descend. Liquidate next lower close greater than ½ sigma.

You may liquidate before any three day holiday on any flimsy excuse, especially if you have a big profit

Once you have liquidated a large position with a huge profit, stay out for a while, maybe three weeks, then start again small.

When you are confused and seem in limbo get out. When you are about to leave town and go on a vacation get out of your positions. When you are about to leave town and you are trying everything you can to stay with your position, you may very well have become a victim of greed.

When you are determined to stay with a position after listening to all the worlds' verbal garbage, and your price is in a sideways gyration, concentrate on getting out at good prices.

MISCELLANEOUS CONSIDERATIONS

TWELVE

LETS GET GOING

If you have lots of experience in trading futures contracts you may not need to read this chapter.

To get started you need to open an account with a Futures Commission Merchant. (FCM) Some have very low commissions and you make all the decisions by yourself.

With others you will have a personal broker who must charge you a larger commission in order to make a living. The commission you pay will be worth it if you have picked a knowledgeable broker. Preferably one who has been in the business awhile, an old pro. You will talk to this person almost every day. He or she will have lots of suggestions on what to trade and what to buy and sell. This then will be a great educational experience. Use very little money and start to trade a little so you learn the words and culture. It will be fun and you may make or lose a little money.

Pick the brains of your broker. Ask lots of questions and get understanding. Do not overtrade. The broker makes money when you buy or sell so do not act on every suggestion, yet do enough trading so he talks to you every day.

Save your real money for the GCP. If you stay with the same broker, he will get very nervous of large pyramided positions. You might have two or more accounts with different FCMs. Once you start a real campaign, however, it is best not to talk to anybody, so as to not get distracted from the main thing.

Your FCM can usually make available to you a software trading platform so that you can buy and sell from your own PC or computer device. You should be able to get a commodity data stream from the FCM from which you can make your calculations. There are also data stream providers that will provide you the data for a fee.

THIRTEEN

IN PERSUIT OF THE GREAT WHITE WHALE

It's a white whale, I say --- a white whale.
Skin your eyes for him, men:
look sharp for white water;
if ye see but a bubble, sing out.

Avast, in the dim,
yonder to the rim,
a spout,
ye lubbers, shout!

Launch the quest,
Careful, count the risk.
Ready the 'poons;
make liquid the rope.

Reach deep within ye;
rouse courage,
confidently approach the yawning abyss;
when ready do not miss.

Wait for the moment,
a gentle roll.
Pounce and thrust with all your might;
yet, if a miss, quickly hide.

HOW TO GET RICH QUICK

Now! Drive it deep!
Hang on for the ride.
watch to cut the rope
when a sound for the deep.

Men! He's coming our way.
Drive another deep,
and another on the rise,
and more and more!

We've got him!
Careful now,
keep the trim,
not sideways to the wind.

Ah! The great taste of success!
Euphoria, pride, guilt
 --- satiated.
Oh! By such we be seized

Moby dives!
Cut the ropes!
Cast off all.
We be had!

Count the survivors.
Any left?
The deep is black indeed.
We've seen the elephant.

Indeed a futures campaign with huge profits and the emotions involved
is really a vision of the elephant. "See the elephant", for those of you
who have not encountered this euphemism is a term from early North
American explorers where being out in the American Wilderness quite

a time and surviving was counted as, "Seeing the elephant."

The Ahab tale, that about the quest of the pursuit of the great white whale, some have postulated, is a complex description of evil insanity. Understand that some will think you too have embarked on an insanity trip. Well, GOOD LUCK, keep cool, and have fun.

FOURTEEN

PARTING THOUGHTS

As you continue in your quest to develop your understanding of markets and develop trading skill you will encounter vast technological change. Technological change is to a great extent unpredictable. The immediate path into the future is the extension of the present. This is called trend. Prognosticators and predictors rely on what they perceive as the trend, and base their predictions on what they think is the present situation, and the extension of that into the future based on what they estimate to be the present trend.

But as time continues, along comes something not really anticipated; a paradigm shift in what was the trend occurs. Over the years I personally benefited to a great extent by technological change by riding the crest of change events and innovation. I very early in my professional career became involved in computers and worked hard at using them to do sundry things. In all of my imagination I never even dreamed some of the things that eventually happened by the use of the computer technology I was even then myself creating. I was one of the first to display data from computers on cathode ray tubes, but never even imagined the present extension of that technology into the laptop computer on which I write these words. I never even anticipated or thought of such a thing.

So you who will use the information in this book, will in the future encounter unbelievable technological change. However, there are fundamental principles of physics such as, for example, electromagnetism, that will not change. So too, the fundamental interacting statistical phenomena of prices of goods in the marketplace will not change. Astounding new uses of the physics of electromagnetism can be employed to develop and make new devices based on the understanding of the physics of electromagnetism. So also, new methods of dealing with market pricing will also appear and come to pass. You as a marketplace profiteer must be aware of these changes and use them to your advantage.

High speed trading and other present methods deployed by very fast diversified computer network resources will affect the marketplace. Ultimately, however, the payoff for you is buying low and selling high, or for shorts, selling high and buying back low. That methodology will not change. Complicated derivatives and algorithmic methods that seem impossible to understand will appear. The human mind is very imaginative in coming up with ways to make a profit and create a benefit.

Nevertheless, in all of this, the statistical theoretical understanding of the marketplace will not change. As long as there are buyers and sellers and the need to balance the consumption of goods with the production of goods, so as to not have a shortage or too abundant a surplus, you will have markets based on statistics. Thus prices will fluctuate to balance the production of producers with the consumption of consumers. The fundamental principles of statistics as presented in this book to understand the pricing of products, will not change.

Collectivist movements, governments, and kingdoms over the centuries have attempted to set the price of goods and create monopolies to so as to have great economic benefits to the few manipulators. Many ugly wars have been fought over controlling pricing, production, and consumption. This seems to have been a main engagement activity of humankind.

The price manipulators succeed for a season, and then new technology or a new military or political force comes along and changes things. Then new pricing occurs, or new production happens, or new demand develops. To a great extent these changes are unpredictable. Thus you must be ready with your money dried out to take advantage of a fundamental price change.

So you as a speculator must adapt. Huge profits can happen and will occur for those prepared when a large pricing change occurs. That is what you are looking for. In my lifetime huge profit opportunity occurred, for example, when the Soviet wheat crop failure happened, when drought occurred in the Midwestern part of the United States, when a hedging contest developed between two very large US grain exporters in 1977, when the corn blight hit the Midwest, when dollar inflation pushed gold prices to unanticipated heights, and when the Hunt brothers attempted to corner the silver market. These examples are just a few. Events like those examples can make you a lot of money and you can become rich in the process of trading futures contracts based on commodities and financial futures instruments.

However, just as kingdoms, governments, and huge business entities, have attempted to control prices, production, and consumption, so modern government manipulators will make the attempt to control because of the political demands of their humankind constituents. Yet the attempt to control will not in the long run work. Humankind manipulation of prices is destined eventually to fail. Governments, however, have tremendous power and can make a powerful mess of everything. This is where you will make a profit. Government manipulators lie. Understand that. You must attempt to identify and understand their lies. Government lies and government attempts to set unsustainable prices are a huge opportunity for you to make a very nice fat profit.

In the 1960s the coin money of the United States was based on silver. Dollar inflation occurred. The government price of silver was $1.29 per ounce and the government attempted to keep the price there by selling the huge horde of government silver. What a fantastic opportunity to make a huge profit. One just knew the government would lose that battle. I watched a cadre of very young Stanford University graduate students, some of them boy wonders not even yet in their 20s, borrow British Pounds (The Brits thought periodically devaluating their pound would lead to prosperity) and buy silver and silver futures contracts. They made a fortune right before my very eyes. I was astounded. They took their fortune and went to Wall Street.

That is one thing you are always looking for – government stupidity!

Another great opportunity for profit is war and the anticipation of war. In the early months of 1979 the commodity markets started to rise, all of them. Nobody knew the reason. The trading system put my clients into grains, metals, almost everything. The rise was becoming spectacular. Then the Red Army of China invaded Viet Nam. The markets exploded upward. Then the Chinese called the war off, went back home, and the markets collapsed. My clients made an astounding amount of profit even though they gave half of it back when the Chinese quit the war. This event contributed to some of my money raising brokers calling me a legend, even in my own time.

The markets predict. Prior to an Israeli/Arab war the markets rose for six weeks or so. Then Israel went to war on a week end. On Monday the markets collapsed. What happened? Three days later the news comes out that the Israeli air force had attacked Egyptian airplanes on the ground at Egyptian air bases, and there were pictures of Egyptian airplanes all lined up with cannon fire holes in the sides of them. The war was over. The market revealed what was about to happen -- revealed it to anybody who wanted to really know anything at all about the possible war and the preparations for war.

Let me insert here a quote from Walter Bagehot in his "Essay on Edward Gibbon".

> 'Much has been written about panics and manias, much more than with the most outstretched intellect we are able to follow or conceive; but one thing is certain, that at particular times a great deal of stupid people have a great deal of stupid money. . . . . At intervals, from causes which are not to the present purpose, the money of these people --- the blind capital, as we call it, of the country --- is particularly large and craving; it seeks for someone to devour it, and there is a "plethora", it finds someone, and there is "speculation", it is devoured, and there is "panic."'

Yes, every once in a while there is blind capital waiting to be devoured. This is you opportunity. Watch and be ready for manias. You will probably not believe what the market is doing. It may look crazy. There will be, however, the opportunity for you to make a ton of money.

You will not be able to use the principles presented in this book as a cookie cutter operation. You will have to adapt and apply your own understanding. The principles are sound but the application may need to be modified as the need arises. You will need to study what is happening in the markets. Day to day and week after week of pricing stuff can become very boring when nothing significant is happening. If you are trying to trade and your money is involved, however, it is not boring. But you must be involved in order to understand the opportunity when the opportunity comes along.

Consider a little past world history and how fortunes were made in the past. Fortunes are essentially built on change. A new technology, a new discovery, a new way of doing things --- this is what makes for profit or fortune. Discovery of gold deposits, railroad and steel barons in the 1800s, electronic devices in the 1950s, copying technology in the 60s, corporate mergers in the 50s and 60s, de-conglomeration and leverage buy outs in the 80s. All based on change about to happen. The Spaniards plundered the Americas; the British and Dutch made fortunes on shipping and trading. There is no end to examples as to how fortunes were made.

As soon as somebody gets good at something and makes a small fortune, competitors move in and the business is no longer as profitable as it once was. Managers take over and the lowest cost producer survives. It is very tough for a speculator to make money in such markets.

Success to a great extent is based on luck and opportunity, and having the will, knowledge, and resources to seize the opportunity. Futures markets have built into them the whole idea of change. Anticipation of bad weather, drought, war, inflations, earthquakes, new discoveries, etc. are already built into these markets. This described trading system sits there waiting for an opportunity. The methods presented herein are complex, esoteric, and have been kept secret. This systematic approach works, and has worked for many years. This system has elements of game theory. In gaming one is always optimizing his tactics and strategies depending on his opponent's moves; in this case, the opponent is market development. This process is dynamic, and, therefore, one continuously adjusts to new factors in the struggle.

Some have asked the question about the morality of speculation. Understand that speculators play a very valuable role in the operation of our wonderful modern civilization. The speculators job is to assume the risk of price fluctuation.

Grains are a very good example of the function of futures markets. Grains are grown during the summer and harvested in the late summer and fall in the United States. Thus grains must be inventoried in order to have plenty to eat year around by livestock and people. Exporters, bread, and cereal manufacturers in the business to provide these foods would be taking great risks to their business if they could not hedge in the futures markets and set the price of their inventory or future needs - - thus the futures market. Futures markets transfer the risk of price fluctuation from producers, inventory holders, and consumers to speculators. Thus speculators are sorely needed and are very valuable to the economy and community health of the United States of America.

The prices of almost all the raw materials and raw foods that are used or consumed in the United States are set on the futures markets. The price of grains, meats, metals, crude, gasoline, natural gas, etc., etc. are all set on the futures trading markets. Speculative interests are required for these markets to operate properly.

Speculators often subsidize the consumers and producers. There have been studies done in the old days of prices averaged over many years of data of the wheat price at London ports versus the price of wheat in the United States. These studies have shown the price of grain on the average has been cheaper in London than in the US. How is that possible since it costs money to ship the grain to England? The speculators have subsidized the grain price in London, and by that, the speculators have subsidized the English bread eaters!

You too will lose money in speculating. In fact, government statistics have shown that most speculators in the futures markets lose money. Thus speculators are a very valuable part of the economic system and you as a speculator are very welcome to participate.

Speculators participate because in the long run they expect, and have high hopes, to make money to cover all their losses and then some. That indeed does happen once in a while, and the cleaver, well-disciplined, talented ones will indeed make lots and lots of money. .

Well enjoy your quest.

APPENDIX

BOOKS MAYBE TO READ

Some books I have found helpful for understanding futures markets, pricing mechanisms, and speculator opportunity are:

View Points of a Commodity Trader, by Roy W. Longstreet

Extraordinary Popular Delusions and the Madness of Crowds, Charles Mackay

The Psychology of Consciousness, by Robert E. Ornstein

The Art of War, Sun Tzu

If you want to become really properly educated for your pursuit of Commodity Futures Riches, go obtain a PhD in Operations Research from Stanford University.

On the other hand if the thought of Stanford makes your stomach churn, or if it gets you discouraged, or if you are an "Ole Blue", bring up, "The Play", on the internet and watch Cal accomplish the impossible running the football through the Stanford Band to victory!